D1736780

WHO WE ARE

THE HISPANIC AMERICAN EXPERIENCE

Barbara Sheen

ReferencePoint Press™

San Diego, CA

About the Author

Barbara Sheen is the author of 111 books for young people. She lives in New Mexico with her family. In her spare time she likes to swim, garden, walk, cook, and read.

For more information, contact:
ReferencePoint Press, Inc.
PO Box 27779
San Diego, CA 92198
www.ReferencePointPress.com

LIBRARY OF CONGRESS CATALOGING-IN-PUBLICATION DATA

Names: Sheen, Barbara, author.
Title: The Hispanic American experience / by Barbara Sheen.
Description: San Diego, CA : ReferencePoint Press, Inc., 2023. | Series:
  Who we are | Includes bibliographical references and index.
Identifiers: LCCN 2022040539 (print) | LCCN 2022040540 (ebook) | ISBN
  9781678204709 (library binding) | ISBN 9781678204716 (ebook)
Subjects: LCSH: Hispanic Americans--Social conditions--Juvenile literature.
  | Hispanic Americans--Ethnic identity--Juvenile literature. | United
  States--Race relations--History--Juvenile literature. | United
  States--Ethnic relations--History--Juvenile literature.
Classification: LCC E184.S75 S48 2023 (print) | LCC E184.S75 (ebook) |
  DDC 305.868/073--dc23/eng/20220915
LC record available at https://lccn.loc.gov/2022040539
LC ebook record available at https://lccn.loc.gov/2022040540

CONTENTS

HISPANIC AMERICANS: BY THE NUMBERS

Total Population
- 62.1 million identify as Hispanic or Latino
- 20.3 million identify as Hispanic or Latino in combination with another ethnic group

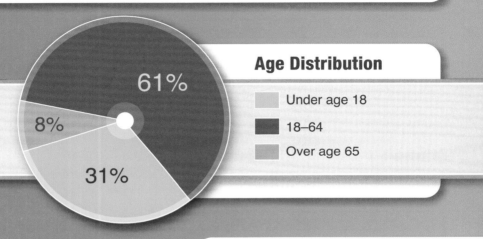

Age Distribution
- Under age 18
- 18–64
- Over age 65

61%
8%
31%

Education
- High school diploma: 74.2%
- Bachelor's degree or higher: 20.6%

Life Expectancy
- Both men and women, 77.9 years
- For women, 81.3 years
- For men, 74.6 years

Five Largest Origin Groups

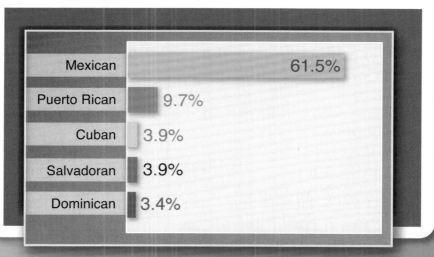

Mexican	61.5%
Puerto Rican	9.7%
Cuban	3.9%
Salvadoran	3.9%
Dominican	3.4%

Median Household Income

- $55,321

Ten States with Largest Hispanic American Populations

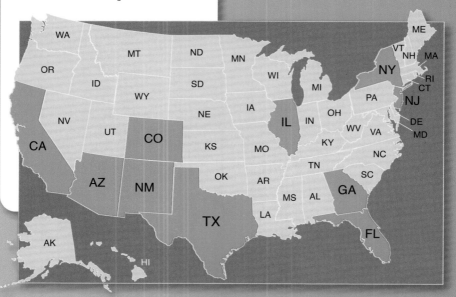

Sixty-Two Million Strong

Juan Antiles, who uses the professional name LeJuan James, is a comedian, author, and social media influencer with more than 2.4 million followers on Instagram and 3.3 million followers on Facebook. The son of a Dominican mother and Puerto Rican father, James spent his early years in Puerto Rico. When he was seven years old, his family moved to Orlando, Florida. Since his first language was Spanish, starting in a new school with a new language was a real challenge for him. Nevertheless, he picked up English quickly, made friends, and adjusted to life in Orlando.

As he became more exposed to American culture, James realized that his family and their traditional Hispanic culture and values made his life and his experiences different from that of his non-Hispanic friends. He recalls:

> Middle school was when I started to understand what it meant to be Hispanic, what made us different from my American friends and their families, like how we greet each other, what we eat, the rules we must obey at home, and the expectation our parents have of us. . . . I also began to realize that when I hung out with my Hispanic friends at their homes, there was a common thread among us all, regardless of what country we came from, and it felt more like home. It was an awakening of sorts.[1]

James used his experiences to create humorous videos about Hispanic life in America. These videos struck a chord with many other Hispanic Americans who, like James, embrace their Hispanic roots.

Young and Growing

The term *Hispanic* is used to describe an ethnic group composed of people who were born in or whose parents or ancestors were born in a Spanish-speaking nation, no matter their race. The terms *Latino* and *Latina*, are also used to describe Hispanics, with *Latino* referring to males and *Latina* to females. According to a recent Pew Research Center Survey, 54 percent of Hispanics have no preference on which of these terms is used to describe them. A more recent, gender-neutral term, *Latinx* is also used, but according to the Pew Research Center, only 3 percent of Hispanics have adopted it. In addition, some Mexican Americans refer to themselves as Chicanos.

The 2020 US Census reports that there are approximately 62 million Hispanics living in the United States. About 86 percent were born in the United States, while 7 percent are naturalized citizens, and 7 percent are noncitizens. As a group, Hispanics are the largest minority in the nation, making up almost 19 percent of the total population, or about one in every five people. Hispanics are also the fastest-growing youth population and the youngest ethnic group in the nation. Indeed, NBC News reports that 1 million Hispanics are projected to turn eighteen each year in the period from 2018 through 2038.

"Middle school was when I started to understand what it meant to be Hispanic, what made us different from my American friends and their families, like how we greet each other, what we eat, the rules we must obey at home, and the expectation our parents have of us."[1]

—LeJuan James, a social media influencer

Three generations of a Hispanic American family celebrate their time together.

A Diverse Group

Hispanics are a diverse group. They can trace their roots to more than twenty nations and are members of every racial group, and many identify as multiracial. These differences affect their experiences and the way they perceive the world. Their nation of origin, for instance, impacts elements of their culture, as well as the reason why they or their ancestors originally came to the United States and the way they got here. According to the 2020 US Census, at about 62 percent, or about 37 million people, Mexicans make up the largest Hispanic group in the United States. Puerto Ricans rank second, with approximately 5.85 million people; while at 2.38 million, Cubans rank third. Other Hispanic groups with at least 1 million US residents include Salvadorans, Dominicans, Guatemalans, Colombians, and Hondurans.

Their race, too, is significant. Afro-Hispanics, for example, face many of the same issues that Black Americans face. They report dealing with higher levels of prejudice and discrimination than White Hispanics.

Where they live also affects their experiences. Although Hispanics live all over the United States, 70 percent of the total Hispanic population lives in five states: California, Texas, Florida, New York, and Arizona. Their experience living in these states, where they are likely to live near others who share their culture, is quite different from that of Hispanics who live in states like Maine or Mississippi, where few other Hispanics reside. Whether they are immigrants, or first-, second-, or later generation Americans also makes a difference in their experiences. Yet even with all these differences, all Hispanics share parts of their culture and history, including the challenges they face, their language, and their close family ties. As James says, "Each Latin American country beyond our own is part of our extended family, sharing similar struggles, and celebrations, and an unbreakable bond."[2]

> "Hispanics are now one of the most influential communities in the United States and the world."[3]
>
> —BeLatina, a website dedicated to Hispanic culture

Challenges and Power

Despite their numbers, living in the United States has not always been easy for Hispanics. They often face prejudice and unfair treatment. Many also deal with language barriers. Nevertheless, their numbers make America's Hispanic population a force to be reckoned with. "Hispanics are now one of the most influential communities in the United States and the world," an article on BeLatina, a website dedicated to Hispanic culture, explains. "Today there are Latinos almost everywhere: in state legislatures, on corporate boards, in the military. . . . Our decisions affect choices, market trends and, obviously, the workforce."[3] Moreover, as the fastest-growing youth population and the youngest ethnic group in the nation, they will almost certainly continue to be instrumental in shaping American society culturally, economically, and politically well into the future.

CHAPTER ONE

Coming to America

Hector is an elderly Mexican American who has lived in southern New Mexico all his life. His ancestors were Spanish colonists who settled in the region in the seventeenth century. Like many other Hispanics, his family has lived in the Southwest ever since. Many Americans are unaware of the long history of Hispanics in America. Some even question their right to be here.

A Unique Situation

Like the rest of the United States, the American Southwest was first inhabited by Native Americans. It became part of the Spanish empire in the sixteenth century. Shortly thereafter, Spanish settlers, missionaries, and soldiers colonized the region. They built forts, missions, and villages in what are now Mexico and the American Southwest. Many intermarried with the native population.

When Mexico won its independence from Spain in 1821, the area fell under Mexican control. Most of the region, which extended from Texas to Northern California, was ceded to the United States at the conclusion of the Mexican-American War in 1848. As part of the acquisition, the US government granted the Mexican residents of the newly acquired territory American citizenship and guaranteed their property rights. Despite these promises and a long presence in the Southwest, the Hispanic citizens were frequently treated as if they were unwelcome foreigners who had no legal rights. As Fatima Garza, a Mexican American woman whose family has lived in Texas for generations, points out, "We didn't cross the border, the border crossed us. So, there's this very unique experience."[4] Indeed, many Hispanics lost their land, businesses, and social status due to illegal acts perpetrated by the newcomers.

Crossing the Southern Border

Most Hispanics arrived in the United States in later centuries. Until the late nineteenth century, the borders were unsecured and no visas or passports were required to enter. As more restrictive policies were enacted, obtaining permission to immigrate to the United States became more difficult. The Department of Homeland Security reports that about 13 percent of Hispanics in the United States are undocumented, meaning they entered the country illegally or overstayed their visas. Many of these individuals live their lives as Americans—working, paying taxes, and sending their kids to school. Many hope to eventually become US citizens.

Whatever their immigration status, most immigrants come to the United States in search of a better life. Many flee poverty, oppression, violence, natural disasters, or political crises. "Our life in Mexico was filled with poverty and strenuous work," a Mexican immigrant recalls, "and everyone had heard that America was the dreamland and that things were different there, so I wanted to get it for myself. I also figured that if I ever had kids, I would hate for them to grow up the way that I did."[5]

For these immigrants, the decision to come to the United States was not an easy one. Most of these newcomers left behind their extended family, friends, and possessions to come to a country where they were unfamiliar with the language and culture and where they were not always welcome. Many, especially those coming from Mexico and Central America, entered the United States via

"Our life in Mexico was filled with poverty and strenuous work, and everyone had heard that America was the dreamland and that things were different there, so I wanted to get it for myself."[5]

—A Mexican immigrant

11

the US-Mexico border, which remains a popular crossing point for Hispanic immigrants today.

For people who seek to enter the United States without permission, the journey to the US-Mexico border and attempts to cross there are filled with danger. Many people hike through long stretches of desert without adequate supplies. Beto, an undocumented Mexican immigrant, faced such a challenge on his journey to the Arizona border. As his son describes, "It took 8 days to cross the desert, the journey was a perilous one, he ran out of food and water, the temperature was extremely high. . . . He would often bump into cacti on his way through the desert. He would end up having over 300 thorns throughout his legs. His shoes were torn apart, his feet ached with huge bumps all over them."[6]

Once immigrants reach the border, getting across can also be challenging. To enter legally through official border crossings, immigrants must have special visas, which are difficult to obtain. Undocumented individuals who are fleeing persecution in their home country may apply for asylum. If asylum is granted, they are allowed

At the conclusion of the Mexican-American War in 1848, a large expanse of territory stretching from Texas to Northern California was ceded to the United States by Mexico.

legal entry and granted protected legal status. But being granted asylum is not easy. Many cases are denied. Asylum seekers go through a screening process to determine whether they have "credible fear" of persecution if they are returned to their home country. If their claim is found plausible, they must undergo a hearing in an immigration court. It takes months before a hearing is scheduled. In the interim, some individuals are released into the United States and monitored by Global Positioning System ankle bracelets. Others are kept in detention facilities. Once a hearing is held, individuals who are not granted asylum are subject to deportation.

Lacking visas or the possibility of acquiring asylum status, some immigrants purchase fraudulent documents in hopes of getting across the border. Others try to slip across without being apprehended by US Border Patrol agents. Many immigrants report trying to get across multiple times before getting through. Amairany Fuentes, a woman whose parents brought her to the United States from Mexico when she was four years old, recalls her experience: "We traveled to the northern Mexican border and attempted many times to cross [into] the US through the desert. . . . As a 4 year old I thought we were going on very long hikes. . . . What I hadn't realized was that we were trying to cross for over a month."[7]

Political Exiles

Other Hispanics made their way to the United States via sea and air. Many members of this group identify as political exiles from Cuba and, more recently, Venezuela. Researchers at the University of Miami found that since 2014 more than two hundred thousand Venezuelans fleeing that nation's repressive government have relocated to South Florida. Researchers also estimate that 1.5 million

Seeking a Better Life

Juan fled Nicaragua in 1989 at age twenty-five. At that time Nicaragua was plagued by war and poverty. Dreaming of a better life, Juan decided to go to the United States. He was undocumented but hoped to be granted asylum due to the turmoil in his home country.

His journey was arduous. As he recalls:

I flew from Managua, Nicaragua to Guatemala because no visa was necessary. From Guatemala, I took buses all the way to Mexico until arriving in Matamoros, Mexico. We only travelled by bus at night because it was safer. Mexican immigration officers would stop you and take your money during the day. A coyote [smuggler] picked us up in Matamoros and took us across the Rio Grande to Brownsville, TX. We were caught by border patrol who took us to a detention center . . . where I spent a month.

Juan was fortunate. He was eventually granted political asylum. He traveled to New York City, where he found work, married, had children, and was able to lead the life that he had dreamed about. Many thousands of other asylum seekers and undocumented immigrants hope for a similar outcome. It is far from being guaranteed, but still they wait.

Quoted in Amy Prado, "Freedom to Think," Made into America, February 18, 2022. https://madein toamerica.org.

Cubans have relocated to the United States since the Cuban Revolution ended in 1959. Their journey, too, was often quite perilous.

Cuban exiles started arriving in large numbers in 1960 after a Communist government, allied with the Soviet Union, seized power on the island. Many of these early arrivals were prosperous individuals whose businesses and property were confiscated by the new government. They traveled to Miami via commercial airlines. Upon their arrival, they were given temporary protection status, which allows individuals from designated countries to legally live and work in the United States until conditions in their home country improve.

At the time, the Cold War was raging. Tension between Cuba and the United States caused the two nations to sever formal diplomatic relations in 1961. As a result, commercial flights between the two nations were banned, and the Cuban government declared travel to the United States a crime. Nevertheless, thousands of desperate Cubans turned to the open sea to escape the new government. Hoping to reach Key West, Florida, 123 miles (198 km) away, these individuals slipped out of Cuba on makeshift rafts. The rafters risked capsizing and drowning or being pursued, captured, and incarcerated by Cuban authorities. Those who reached US waters were given safe haven. In fact, more than six thousand Cubans were admitted into Florida from 1962 to 1965.

Then in 1965, in a rare act of cooperation between the United States and Cuba, an airlift program known as Freedom Flights was created. The program was paid for and organized by the US government. It lasted eight years, bringing about 300,000 more Cubans to Florida. When the freedom flights ended, the Cuban government again barred islanders from traveling to the United States. But in April 1980, facing economic problems, the Cuban government announced that anyone who wanted to relocate to another country was free to leave Cuba via Mariel Harbor, Havana. In response, Cuban Americans organized a boatlift to transport

Lacking required documents to enter the United States legally, some migrants cross the border in remote areas, in order to avoid capture by Border Patrol agents.

their former compatriots to Florida. More than 125,000 Cubans, who came to be called "Marielitos," arrived in Florida before the program ended in September 1980.

The Marielitos' journey was not easy. Most of the vessels were old, leaky, and jam-packed. High seas and severe storms were common. Quite a few boats sank. US Marine helicopters pulled survivors out of the water and brought them to shore, but an unknown number of Marielitos drowned or were killed by sharks. Maydel Santana Bravo recalls her experience of this journey: "We are on this shrimping boat full of people . . . then a 24-hour ordeal started. Very bad weather, the darkest ocean I've ever seen in my life, waves that came over the boat. . . . It was a rather terrifying ordeal."[8]

For some, the ordeal did not end when they set foot on dry land. Many Marielitos had family members waiting for them in Miami. But others were not so fortunate. They wound up waiting in tent cities that were set up to hold them until they could be resettled.

Fourteen years passed before the Cuban government again allowed people to leave the island. Lacking any other means of transportation, tens of thousands of Cuban refugees fled their homeland on makeshift rafts, inner tubes, and sailboards in what became known as the Cuban rafter or *balsero* crisis. Fearing the massive exodus would overwhelm the United States, yet still wanting to help the immigrants, President Bill Clinton established a policy known as wet foot, dry foot. It allowed Cubans who reached US soil to stay in the country while sending those who were intercepted at sea back to Cuba.

The wet foot, dry foot policy ended in 2017, two years after Cuba and the United States

"We are on this shrimping boat full of people . . . then a 24-hour ordeal started. Very bad weather, the darkest ocean I've ever seen in my life, waves that came over the boat. . . . It was a rather terrifying ordeal."[8]

—Maydel Santana Bravo, a Cuban immigrant

A Cuban refugee family arrives in Miami in 1966. Starting in 1965, under a program lasting eight years, the US government allowed approximately three hundred thousand Cubans to move to Florida from their native land.

renewed diplomatic relations. Since then Cubans have been required to enter the United States through a port of entry like immigrants from other countries. Nonetheless, Cubans continue to flee the island in large numbers. Many fly to Nicaragua, then travel overland to the US-Mexico border, where they claim asylum. According to US Customs and Border Protection, from October 2021 to April 2022, approximately 115,000 Cubans arrived at the southern border. The majority were allowed entry.

Already Citizens

Unlike Cubans and other Hispanic immigrants, Puerto Ricans do not have to worry about borders and immigration. They are US citizens. From the landing of Columbus in 1492 until 1898, Puerto Rico belonged to Spain. It became a US territory in 1898

Puerto Ricans in Hawaii

In the early twentieth century, landowners in Hawaii recruited Puerto Rican laborers to work on Hawaiian sugar plantations. An article on Big Island Now, a Hawaiian news website, describes the workers' month-long journey and their life in Hawaii:

> In November 1900, the first group of Puerto Ricans—54 men—set out to make the long journey to Hawai'i. The trip was long and grueling. They sailed from San Juan harbor to New Orleans, Louisiana, then rode the train all the way to Los Angeles, California. From there, they sailed to Hawai'i on the steamship. . . . While they had hoped to make a better life for themselves and their families, the early days of working in Hawai'i was not pleasant or easy. With minimal immigration laws in place in the territory of Hawai'i, the Puerto Ricans found themselves being treated very poorly—in some cases, they were even starved by the plantation owners. Despite all the hardships, within less than a year, 5,000 Puerto Rican men, women and children had made their way to Hawai'i and established themselves on four islands.
>
> Today approximately forty thousand Puerto Ricans live in Hawaii. Many are descendants of these plantation workers.

Big Island Now, "How Puerto Ricans Arrived on Hawai'i Island," September 6, 2017. https://big islandnow.com.

after the Spanish-American War. In 1917 Congress passed a law that gave anyone born in Puerto Rico US citizenship. Therefore, Puerto Ricans can enter, travel freely, and live anywhere in the United States, just like other citizens. They can also join the military, access certain social services, and vote in local elections on the island. However, they cannot vote in national elections unless they live in and register to vote in one of the fifty states.

Even though Puerto Ricans had become US citizens, before World War II, Puerto Rican migration to the mainland was slow. After the war ended, however, things changed. The island was plagued by high unemployment and widespread poverty. Therefore, the US government encouraged Puerto Ricans to migrate to the mainland, where jobs were plentiful. In addition, affordable air travel had recently become available, making it easy for thousands of Puerto Ricans to relocate.

Many of these individuals considered their relocation temporary. Like many Puerto Ricans today, they intended to move back to the island when they had saved enough money to rebuild their lives there. Here is how writer and community activist Bernardo Vega describes this plan: "First savings would be for sending for close relatives. Years later the time would come to return home with pots of money. Everyone's mind was on that farm they'd be buying or the business they'd set up in town. . . . All of us were building our own little castles in the sky."[9]

Continuing economic problems in Puerto Rico—including extreme weather events such as Hurricane Maria, which devastated the island in 2017—have kept many Puerto Ricans from moving back to the island. Moreover, many have adjusted to life in the states and accept the United States as their permanent home. In fact, there are currently more Puerto Ricans living on the mainland than on the island itself. Nevertheless, since travel between Puerto Rico and the continental United States has become relatively cheap and easy, it is not unusual for mainland Puerto Ricans to go back and visit the island frequently. Indeed, some feel they have the best of both worlds.

That is not to say that Puerto Rican life on the mainland is ideal. Although they are US citizens, like other Hispanic Americans, they are often treated like outsiders who do not belong there. Clearly, for all Hispanics, coming to the United States and starting a new life is not easy. But the dream of liberty, opportunity, and a better life gives individuals the courage to face the challenge.

CHAPTER TWO

Striving for Rights

When Mexican American civil rights activist Carmen Perez was a teenager growing up in California, she had a troubling encounter with the police. Her brother was driving Perez and her teammates home from their high school basketball game when they were pulled over by the police for a minor infraction. The teens, all of whom were Hispanic, Black, or Asian, had done nothing serious enough to warrant the treatment they received. Perez recalls, "I'll never forget the police officers making my brother get out of the car with his hands up and then throwing him to the ground, hog-tying him at gunpoint right in front of me and all my teammates. Then the police made all of us put up our hands, and we were escorted to sit on the curb at gunpoint."[10]

Perez attributes the incident to racism. Such incidents are not unusual. Even though there are federal and state laws that protect people against discrimination, Hispanic Americans frequently face prejudice and unjust treatment in multiple areas of their lives.

Striving to Mend an Unfair Criminal Justice System

Discriminatory treatment of Hispanics by law enforcement is a long-standing problem. In fact, in the past, Hispanics were victims of vigilante violence, which was often sanctioned by some police agencies. From the mid-1800s until the early twentieth century, Hispanic landowners and laborers residing in the Southwest were frequent targets of mob violence. Some White settlers, motivated by prejudice and the desire to seize

Hispanic-owned land and businesses, falsely accused Mexican Americans of a variety of crimes. In reaction to the accusations, angry mobs seized the alleged criminals before they were allowed to stand trial and hanged them in public executions.

A group of researchers at the University of Texas found that it was not unusual for local sheriffs and other law enforcement officials to condone the proceedings. Some even took part in these murders, known as lynchings. Similar violence frequently occurred against Hispanic miners who made mining claims in California during the gold rush era. Historians estimate that at least five hundred Hispanics were lynched in Texas and California before the practice ended.

Nonetheless, even today, Hispanics often face unequal treatment from law enforcement and the courts. According to the American Bar Association, Hispanic first offenders are more likely to be detained before trial than their White counterparts, and the incarceration rate of Hispanics is nearly double that of Whites. Worse yet, Hispanics are frequently victims of police brutality. UnidosUS, a civil rights organization, reports that Hispanics are 1.7 times more likely to be killed by police than White people. From 2014 to May 2021, an estimated 2,653 Hispanics died in police custody or in encounters with the police. One incident involved thirteen-year-old Adam Toledo. He was shot and killed by police during a foot chase in Chicago in 2021. The police claimed the seventh grader was holding a gun when they shot him; however, police body camera video shows the boy unarmed with his hands up.

In addition, in many places police are encouraged to question the immigration status of anyone they stop if they suspect that the person is undocumented. Without any facts to justify suspicions, Hispanics are often targeted for questioning based

"I'll never forget the police officers making my brother get out of the car with his hands up and then throwing him to the ground, hog-tying him at gunpoint right in front of me."[10]

—Carmen Perez, a civil rights activist

on their appearance or the language they speak. This is called racial profiling. US Immigration and Customs Enforcement (ICE) agents, who are authorized to operate within 100 miles (161 km) of US borders, also have the right to stop and question anyone they think may be undocumented. That is what happened to Ana Suda and her friend, both of whom are American citizens. In 2018 they were stopped and questioned by a federal agent in Montana when he overheard them speaking Spanish. "I was so embarrassed," Suda says. "Everybody's looking at you like you're doing something wrong. I don't think speaking Spanish is something criminal. . . . My friend, she started crying. . . . And I told her, we are not doing anything wrong. . . . I just don't want this to happen anymore. I want people to know they have the right to speak whatever language they want."[11]

Suda recorded the incident on her cell phone and contacted the American Civil Liberties Union seeking legal counsel. She is not alone in wanting to fight back. Many Hispanics are striving to end such practices by taking legal action.

Striving for Justice in the Workplace

Others are striving for justice in the workplace. Since the nineteenth century, Hispanic workers have been vital to the US workforce and the national economy. As of 2022 there were approximately 29 million Hispanics in the US workforce. And UnidosUS predicts that by 2030, one out of every five American workers will be Hispanic. Hispanics are employed in every field imaginable. They work as educators, first responders, and in all areas of health care. They work in the justice system, in the hospitality industry, and in high-tech fields, including engineering. Yet despite their numbers and their presence in all sectors of US society, they have often been discriminated against and treated unfairly in the workplace.

Hispanic agricultural workers, for example, have been subjected to substandard working conditions for decades. More than 50 percent of all farmworkers are Hispanic. Of these individuals, about half are undocumented. Historically, farmworkers have been required to work long hours under unhealthy working conditions, for less than a living wage. In 1960, for example, the minimum wage was one

Dolores Huerta, Activist

Dolores Huerta is a civil rights legend who has spent her life working to end economic injustice. Huerta grew up in Stockton, California. Her mother owned a restaurant and a small hotel, where she frequently gave farmworkers free food and lodging. Inspired by her mother, Huerta began fighting for the rights of Hispanic farmworkers as a young woman. She ran voter registration drives, lobbied local elected officials to improve working conditions for farmworkers, and organized nonviolent protests and boycotts. In 1962 she cofounded the United Farm Workers of America union with Cesar Chavez.

In the ensuing years, Huerta's activism has helped many people in the Hispanic community. Her work helped make it possible for Californians to take the driver's license written test in Spanish. And, through the efforts of Huerta and others, federal welfare assistance was extended to needy farmworkers and their families. Her efforts have not come without peril. She was arrested more than twenty times and on one occasion was severely beaten by the police. Yet Huerta has persisted. She has received dozens of honors in recognition of her work, including the Presidential Medal of Freedom, and is a role model to many Hispanic Americans.

dollar per hour, yet farmworkers were paid as little as forty cents per hour. Cesar Chavez, a Mexican American activist, sought to protect farmworkers' rights. From 1965 to 1970, he organized and led a series of strikes by California agricultural workers, most of whom were Hispanic. The laborers walked out on grape growers, demanding better working conditions. As a result, farmworkers were given the right to engage in collective bargaining and later joined the United Farm Workers of America union, which Chavez had cofounded.

Nevertheless, farmworkers still work under difficult conditions for low wages. They are excluded from federal overtime requirements and many occupational health and safety protections. For example, farmworkers are routinely exposed to harmful pesticides that have been linked to cancer, birth defects, and other health problems. Moreover, during the height of the COVID-19 pandemic, farmworkers were disproportionately infected by the virus. So were meat-packers, who are mainly Hispanic and Black. Employers were slow to enact safety measures for both farmworkers and meat-packers that might have helped slow the spread. In fact, in some meat-packing plants, management forced workers with COVID-19 symptoms to come to work. In response, a number of Hispanic advocacy groups have filed civil rights complaints against meat-packing companies.

Hispanic agricultural workers have been subjected to substandard working conditions for decades. These workers, in California, harvest carrots.

Hispanics in white-collar jobs also report experiencing harassment and discrimination in the workplace. They describe being victims of unfair hiring and promotion practices, unequal pay, and racial slurs. A 2021 Gallup poll found that among White and Hispanic job applicants with identical qualifications, White applicants were 24 percent more likely to be given an interview than were Hispanics. Discriminatory practices are especially common when it comes to Hispanic women. In 2021 the Pew Research Center found that Hispanic women with a bachelor's degree earned 35 percent less than White men doing the same jobs with the same qualifications. Even Supreme Court justice Sonia Sotomayor, who is of Puerto Rican descent, has faced discrimination during her career. "In every position that I've been in, there have been naysayers who don't believe I'm qualified or who don't believe I can do the work. And I feel a special responsibility to prove them wrong,"[12] she says.

Battling to End Unjust Deportations

On occasion, when Hispanic workers complain about workplace injustices, their employers retaliate by calling in ICE. Agents conduct workplace raids that intimidate both documented and undocumented individuals. Raids are also conducted in Hispanic communities where families with mixed immigration status often live. The goal of these raids is to identify, detain, and deport undocumented individuals. However, US citizens have also been caught up in these raids. In the process, many have been unjustly detained and even deported. In 1954 the government enacted a mass deportation program called Operation Wetback to address concerns about migration along the southern border. People were snatched from their homes and workplaces, and families were torn apart. Over 2 million Hispanics were deported in the operation, including many American citizens of Hispanic descent.

American citizens have also been caught up in more recent actions. According to a *Los Angeles Times* report, nearly fifteen hundred US citizens were wrongfully detained from 2012 to 2018. Additionally, the US Government Accountability Office

Special Problems Plague Afro-Hispanics

According to the Pew Research Center, there are an estimated 6 million Afro-Hispanics (also called Afro-Latinos) currently living in the United States. Most trace their roots to the Dominican Republic, Cuba, and Puerto Rico. Many are descendants of African slaves who were brought to the Caribbean in the 1500s to work, and sometimes intermarry, for the Spanish colonists.

Afro-Hispanics have been striving for equal rights for a long time. Historically, discrimination against this group has been twofold. They have faced discrimination for being Hispanic as well as for being Black. Compared to lighter-skinned Hispanic Americans, they are less likely to have a college education, and their income is usually lower. And according to the Pew Research Center, people are more likely to question their intelligence. Their experiences are rarely reported by the media.

reports that as many as seventy US citizens were mistakenly deported from 2015 to 2020. The majority of wrongful detentions and deportations involved Hispanics. Wrongful cases include that of Carlos Rios, a US citizen who was arrested on suspicion of immigration violations by ICE agents in Tacoma, Washington, in 2019. Despite explaining that he had been a US citizen for more than twenty years and showing agents his US passport, Rios was imprisoned in a federal facility for a week. Plus, he was held in solitary confinement for some of this time. These actions violated his rights as a citizen. Recalling the experience, Rios says, "I can't understand why they detained me and why no one listened to me. . . . I hope they don't do this to anyone else."[13]

After his release, Rios filed a lawsuit against ICE for unlawful imprisonment. He was awarded $125,000 as part of a settlement agreement. Matt Adams, legal director of Northwest Immigrant Rights Project, which represented Rios, explains that immigration agents "do not have the authority to ar-

"[Immigration and Customs Enforcement agents] do not have the authority to arrest someone based on a hunch or suspicion, and certainly not based on a person's race, ethnicity or apparent language."[14]

—Matt Adams, legal director of Northwest Immigrant Rights Project

rest someone based on a hunch or suspicion, and certainly not based on a person's race, ethnicity or apparent language."[14]

Fighting for Civic Inclusion and Civil Rights

Other injustices that Hispanics have striven to redress are related to civil rights and civil inclusion. Segregation was a problem for Hispanics until the passage of the Civil Rights Act of 1964. Before that time, Hispanics in many parts of the Southwest were barred entry from or forced to sit in separate sections of restaurants and other public establishments patronized by non–Hispanic Americans. Civil rights activist and 2010 Presidential Medal of Freedom winner Sylvia Mendez remembers how her family was refused service in a California restaurant in the 1940s because of their ethnicity. "My father who spoke very good English said, 'Miss, why aren't we being served?' and the waitress said it was because they didn't serve Mexicans there, so we had to get up and leave."[15]

President Barack Obama awards the 2010 Presidential Medal of Freedom to civil rights activist Sylvia Mendez during a White House ceremony.

Around the same time, Mendez was barred from enrolling in a local Orange County, California, public school located near her home. It was for White students only. Based on her surname and skin color, she was assigned to a run-down, inadequately equipped and staffed "Mexican school." Alleging discrimination, her father took the issue to court in the case of *Mendez v. Westminster*. During the trial, school officials insisted that discrimination was not the issue. They claimed that Mexican American students were disease-ridden

27

and mentally inferior to White students and that the school district was protecting the health and education of White students by keeping Hispanic Americans out. Nonetheless, the judge ruled against the school district, maintaining that segregating Hispanic students violated their constitutional rights. Therefore, in 1946 the state of California ended school segregation. Other cases followed in Arizona and Texas. Eight years later, in 1954, the landmark school segregation case of *Brown v. Board of Education* was brought before the US Supreme Court. The court ruled to end school segregation nationally, basing its decision on some of the arguments presented in the *Mendez* case.

> "In the end, the American dream is not a sprint, or even a marathon, but a relay. Our families don't always cross the finish line in the span of one generation. But each generation passes on to the next the fruits of their labor."[16]
>
> —Julian Castro, a Hispanic American politician

However, unjust treatment of Hispanics did not end in 1954. Hispanic Americans, no matter their place of origin, were often prohibited from living in certain neighborhoods, serving on juries, or holding elective office, among other injustices. The passage of the Civil Rights Act of 1964 and the Fair Housing Act of 1968 helped improve things, as did the establishment of a number of advocacy groups such as the Young Lords and La Raza Unida (which has since been renamed UnidosUS). Yet, although they have come a long way, Hispanic Americans still continue to fight for equal rights. As Julián Castro, the former mayor of San Antonio, Texas, and the head of the US Department of Housing and Urban Development in the Obama administration, says, "In the end, the American dream is not a sprint, or even a marathon, but a relay. Our families don't always cross the finish line in the span of one generation. But each generation passes on to the next the fruits of their labor."[16]

CHAPTER THREE

Building Communities

Lissy Suazo is a nineteen-year-old Honduran American whose family moved to Big Sky, Montana, from New York City when she was twelve years old. At that time there were hardly any Hispanic families in the area. She was the first non-English speaker and the second student of color in the local school.

At first, Suazo felt like an outsider in the southwestern Montana town. But over time, she learned English, made friends, and adjusted to her new home. Nonetheless, the transition was not easy. By the time Suazo was in high school, other Hispanic families had moved into the area, drawn by jobs in the resort industry that serves Yellowstone National Park. Remembering how isolated she felt at the start of her life in Big Sky, Suazo went out of her way to welcome the new arrivals. She tutored the new students in English, and she started a Latino student union, which provided them with academic and social support. Plus she created the online Spanish-language newspaper *Noticias Montaña* in an effort to connect Spanish speakers in the region. Suazo's various actions helped build a sense of community among the local Hispanic population, bringing people who felt marginalized together. As Suazo explains, "I always told my mom, 'Mami, I want to change the world,' and what better way to change the world than starting where you are."[17]

What Is a Community?

Through her efforts, Suazo helped plant the seeds from which a new Hispanic community has started to grow. Although many people think of a community as a geographic place such as a

When Lissy Suazo's family moved to the Montana resort town of Big Sky, few Hispanics lived there. As their numbers have grown, her online Spanish-language newspaper has helped create a sense of community.

town or city, not all communities are geographic. In fact, the term *community* has multiple definitions and meanings. It can be used to describe a variety of groups whose members share a common characteristic, interest, or goal and who socially interact with each other. People who live in the same neighborhood or are members of a particular religious congregation, club, support group, or sports team may all be considered a community. So too are those who share a hobby or political affiliation, as well as those who attend the same school or are employed by the same company. Indeed, most people are usually part of multiple communities.

The size of communities also varies. They can be large or small, local, regional, national, or international. And they can be nested, which means a small community may exist within a larger one. But no matter a community's size or makeup, being part of a community gives individuals a feeling of mutual support and belonging. Plus, as a group, community members wield more power than they would individually, which helps them better achieve common goals.

For Hispanic Americans, being part of a welcoming community is especially helpful because they often feel misunderstood by the larger population. They are frequently viewed and treated as "others" by many Americans and may feel unwelcome, misjudged, or secondary as a result. Being part of a community in which members share a common culture, interests, goals, and problems helps them feel connected and empowers them to stand up for their rights.

Large and Small Geographic Communities

Like all communities, Hispanic communities come in all forms. Hispanic geographic communities can be found throughout the United States. Some, like that in Big Sky, are just developing, while many are well established. Generally, people—including recent immigrants—choose to live in communities where they can find employment and affordable housing and where other members of their family or other individuals who share their culture reside. Living near others who share the same culture gives individuals a feeling of normalcy, no matter how different the local culture might be. "You go where your people go,"[18] says Susie Ximenez, a young Mexican American whose family followed friends and relatives to Poughkeepsie, New York.

Although Hispanic geographic communities can be found in smaller cities like Poughkeepsie, the largest and oldest Hispanic communities in the United States are located in or close to large metropolitan areas. Miami, Florida, with a population of more than 1 million Hispanic residents, is one of these large metropolitan areas. Individuals from Cuba, Puerto Rico, the Dominican Republic, and South and Central America all feel comfortable there. The heart of Miami's Hispanic community is a neighborhood located in downtown Miami known as Little Havana. It is one of the largest and most famous Hispanic communities in the United States. About fifty thousand people, most of whom are Cuban exiles, call Little Havana their home. With its espresso stands, Cuban restaurants, art galleries and street art that showcase the works

Colonias

Not all Hispanic communities are located in large metropolitan areas. More than a half million Hispanic Americans live in impoverished communities, known as colonias, that dot the Texas-Mexico border. There are also colonias along the southern borders of Arizona, California, and New Mexico. Colonias are unincorporated communities, located outside of city limits. Many colonias lack basic services that most Americans take for granted, such as paved roads, clean water, wastewater disposal, trash service, internet access, and emergency health care facilities. According to a report by the Federal Reserve Bank of Dallas, about thirty-eight thousand residents of Texas colonias lack access to safe drinking water.

Typically, colonia residents are low-income Hispanics and recent immigrants. Many lack English language skills, which hampers their employability. Yet despite all these challenges, members of different colonias have started organizing their communities in an effort to improve living conditions. They are gradually making progress. For instance, due to the work of one group, public lighting has been installed in eight colonias in Texas's Hidalgo County, making these communities safer.

of Hispanic artists, and nightclubs that feature Cuban-style salsa and rap, Little Havana is considered to be the epicenter of Cuban life and culture in the United States.

It is common to hear Spanish spoken throughout the neighborhood. Many businesses are owned by Hispanics, and most employees are bilingual. Bilingual services are the norm in area houses of worship. The local schools offer bilingual education, and the libraries offer reading material in both English and Spanish. There are many nonprofit organizations in the community that provide resources and services relevant to community members. And the grocery stores sell favorite Cuban staple foods like plantains and yuccas that are hard to find in non-Hispanic communities. It is a community in which Hispanics feel at home. As author Paola Ramos, who grew up in the area, explains, "As a Latino you don't really need to explain who you are. You simply belong."[19]

New York City is another city that is home to multiple Hispanic communities. Approximately 2.4 million Hispanics live in New York City, with many residing in the northern part of the borough of Manhattan and in the southern part of the borough of Bronx. Two neighborhoods in northern Manhattan—Spanish Harlem and Washington Heights—are among the most well known. Also known as El Barrio, Spanish Harlem has the highest concentration of Puerto Rican residents in New York City. In fact, many of the residents call themselves Nuyoricans. Similarly, Washington Heights is home to the largest Dominican population in the world outside of the Dominican Republic. Both communities are filled with sights and smells reminiscent of the Caribbean. Both provide residents with a supportive environment and a sense of belonging. As music executive and fashion designer Caroline Diaz explains, "I'm from Washington Heights . . . and it's a special neighborhood. I call it Little Dominican Republic. It's our own little Hispanic land and heritage."[20]

"I'm from Washington Heights . . . and it's a special neighborhood. I call it Little Dominican Republic. It's our own little Hispanic land and heritage."[20]

—Caroline Diaz, a music executive and fashion designer

Cuban Americans enjoy a game of chess in a section of Miami, Florida, known as Little Havana.

Because they are the majority in these and other Hispanic communities throughout the United States, residents are shielded from much of the prejudice, discrimination, and otherness that Hispanics living in other parts of the nation often face. In fact, some residents deal with culture shock if they relocate to other areas. Says Ramos:

"It's somewhat shocking when you realize that the rest of the country looks, sounds, and feels absolutely nothing like the environment you grew up in."[21]

—Paola Ramos, an author

It's somewhat shocking when you realize that the rest of the country looks, sounds, and feels absolutely nothing like the environment you grew up in. If you grow up thinking that speaking Spanish is the norm and that being from Cuba or Colombia is way more common than being from Ohio or Tennessee, then it's a strange feeling when you realize that's not exactly the case in the rest of the country.[21]

Indeed, many individuals who move out of these communities to live in other parts of the country often return, or they help establish a new Hispanic community in their new home.

Keeping Communities Vital

Whether new or old, or small or large, for communities to thrive they cannot be static. In order to best serve residents, the services, opportunities, and support communities provide must grow and change with the population, events, and times. The efforts of individuals, businesses, schools, and places of worship to adapt and grow with the population help communities remain vital. For instance, since the 1990s many people of Mexican descent have moved into Spanish Harlem. To serve this growing Mexican American community, the local stores have added Mexican food staples like chili peppers and tortillas to their inventory. Similarly, Mexican restaurants and bakeries have opened in the neighborhood. And street festivals that celebrate Mexican holidays have become as much a part of the local scene as those celebrating Puerto Rican culture.

Meeting the needs of millennial and Generation Z Hispanics, who are often more assimilated to American culture than members of older generations, is another way communities stay relevant. For example, like a growing number of other Americans, many Hispanics are embracing a plant-based diet to address ethical, health, and environmental concerns. In response, schools and community centers throughout the United States, including many in Hispanic communities, are offering plant-based alternatives for favorite Hispanic dishes. Vegan substitutes include vegetarian tacos and enchiladas, along with plantain and rice bowls, to name a few.

Local merchants are also adapting. A Mexican American–owned bakery in Pilsen, a large Hispanic community in Chicago, added vegan breads and pastries to its menu to serve the changing tastes of its more socially and health-conscious clientele. The owner has also tried to make the baked goods more appealing to the eye to cater to young customers who like to post photos

Merchants Lead Public Health Efforts

Local merchants do more than offer retail services in Hispanic communities. During times of crisis, especially, they help keep communities strong. For example, in an effort to stem the growing opioid addiction problem in Chicago's Hispanic community, a local café owner started hosting weekly Narcotics Anonymous meetings, as well as holding workshops on the use of naloxone, a medication that helps counter an opioid overdose.

Likewise, during the COVID-19 pandemic, it was not unusual for businesses in Hispanic communities to set up bulletin boards that provided patrons information in English and Spanish about the virus. Some businesses provided free face masks. Others worked in conjunction with the local health department to set up pop-up vaccination sites for residents, many of whom had not been vaccinated due to language barriers or lack of transportation to larger vaccination sites, among other issues. For example, a barbershop in Nashua, New Hampshire, which has a large Hispanic population, helped vaccinate about thirty people a day.

of food online. "People now want to take pictures, so we have to make the breads look cute,"[22] says Xiomara, the bakery's owner.

Like Xiomara's artistic breads, art in many forms helps keep communities relevant. Many Hispanic communities are home to public art in the form of murals, mosaics, and graffiti art that depict the history, culture, and politics of the community. Modern muralists are adding new works, which raise awareness of current issues that the community faces. A 2021 mural in one of San Francisco's Hispanic communities, for example, depicts a young man and his grandmother standing together, wearing face masks. The community was disproportionately hard hit by the COVID-19 virus. The mural serves as a way to honor the strength and courage of local residents during the pandemic, while reminding the young of the importance of taking care of the elderly and of continuing to wear a face mask to combat new variants of the virus.

In many instances, creating new murals is a group effort, with many community members contributing to the project. Often these group projects include the work of children, young adults, and the elderly. Local merchants also get involved by allowing artists to create murals on the outer walls of their businesses. In-

Many Hispanic neighborhoods are home to public art that depicts the history, culture, and politics of the community like this one in San Francisco.

deed, besides depicting local culture and concerns, these group projects also serve to bring people together, thereby strengthening the community.

Organizations Help

Local, state, and national associations also play a key role in building, growing, and keeping communities vital. These groups help Hispanic Americans come together in support of issues that affect them. Hispanic professional organizations and societies, in particular, offer a wide range of activities and events that support and help Hispanic professionals and communities. For example, part of the mission of the National Association of Hispanic Nurses is improving the quality of health care in Hispanic communities, while a focus of the National Association of Hispanic Real Estate Professionals is helping Hispanics find safe and affordable housing.

Other organizations concentrate on improving education in Hispanic communities. Aspira ("aspire" in Spanish) is one of the most well known. It was established in 1961 as a way to better the lives of Puerto Rican students and communities through education. It has since widened its focus to include all Hispanic Americans. The organization has been instrumental in changing the way that Hispanic students are educated by advocating for bilingual classes, more Hispanic educators, textbooks including Hispanic names, and community control of local schools. With chapters in secondary schools in Hispanic communities, Aspira offers services such as free tutoring and information about college opportunities that are aimed at helping students succeed in high school and pursue higher education. In addition, chapter members receive leadership development training, which they use in community service projects that improve and empower their communities.

Clearly, many people and organizations are essential to building, growing, and maintaining Hispanic communities. These communities, in all their different forms, are a vital part of the lives of Hispanic Americans. The communities help preserve their culture, bring them together, and empower them.

CHAPTER FOUR

Holding On to Identity

Ariana DeBose is a Puerto Rican singer, choreographer, dancer, and actress who was born and raised in North Carolina. In 2022 she won a Golden Globe Award and an Academy Award for Best Actress in a Supporting Role. She received both awards for playing the role of Anita, a Puerto Rican immigrant, in the 2021 film remake of *West Side Story*. Yet because she felt somewhat distant from her Puerto Rican heritage and does not speak Spanish, she worried that she was not "Hispanic enough" to play the role. "I thought, for the longest time, that made me less of what I was," she says. "Perhaps I didn't represent the community well enough. And so, when the movie came around, and even just deciding to walk in the room [to audition] I was like, 'I don't know if I'm really what you're looking for. I have the skill set, but maybe my background isn't good enough.'"[23]

Like DeBose, many Hispanic Americans struggle with their identity. They grow up navigating between two cultures and in many cases cannot easily define who they are. Some feel pressure to assimilate into and completely embrace American culture. Others are pressured to cling to their Hispanic roots while excluding their American side. Many walk a fine line, changing their personas to please those around them. In an effort to be accepted, they may modify their speech, appearance, and body language in order to emphasize one side of their culture while excluding the other. In the process, individuals can lose sight of who they are, which makes them feel disconnected from their true selves. Often, they feel like posers who are neither authentic Americans nor authentic Hispanics. According to Honduran American actress, director, and producer America Ferrera, who struggled with her identity, "[There is] this cultural rubber band, with the American side stretching one way and the Latina side stretching the other. There's this tug-of-war between two cultures. Am I Latin? Am I American? What the hell am I?"[24]

As they straddle two worlds and struggle with their identity, some individuals come to feel more connected to and identify with one culture over the other. Others feel that ignoring part of their cultural background denies part of themselves and their history. Many of the latter group identify as bicultural. They accept and embrace their American heritage while maintaining a connection to their Hispanic cultural roots. Indeed, according to a 2021 Telemundo poll, about 62 percent of Hispanic Americans identify as bicultural. Dallas journalist

"[There is] this cultural rubber band, with the American side stretching one way and the Latina side stretching the other. There's this tug-of-war between two cultures."[24]

—America Ferrera, Honduran American actress

Ariana DeBose (in the yellow dress) won an Academy Award for her portrayal of Anita, a Puerto Rican immigrant, in the 2021 remake of West Side Story.

Jatsive Hernandez is one of these individuals. She struggled with her identity for years until, she says:

> I decided to lean in. . . . Instead of feeling embarrassed for mispronouncing a few words, I felt joy at the fact that I could speak two languages fluently. . . . Today instead of carrying shame for being Mexican-American, I carry a sense of purpose. I still sing along to [George] Strait, but now I also sing along to [Vicente] Fernandez. I'm involved in organizations like the Dallas Cotillion Club and also travel to Mexico with my dad to help my abuelito [grandpa] with the bean harvest. . . . Being bicultural has allowed me to be a part of two cultures that fuse to form a third culture, the Mexican-American/Chicano culture.[25]

Language and Identity

Language plays a key role in Hispanic Americans' cultural identity. The Pew Research Center reports that about 86 percent of Hispanic American adults heard Spanish spoken at home while they were growing up and speak Spanish to their children. Nevertheless, though Spanish use is widespread, not all Hispanic Americans are bilingual.

There are various reasons for this. In some cases, after living in the United States for multiple generations, Hispanic families become so acculturated to their new home that they no longer use Spanish. In other cases, individuals who were mistreated for speaking Spanish or teased because of their faulty English do not speak Spanish to their children, as a way to shield them from similar abuse. Some parents do not teach their children Spanish, in the belief that the more their children adhere to American norms, the greater their chances of being accepted and succeeding in American society.

Being or not being bilingual sometimes affects the way Hispanics view themselves and one another. Many limited-Spanish speak-

Speaking Spanglish

Many Hispanic Americans mix Spanish and English words and phrases in their conversations. They are said to be speaking "Spanglish." Spanglish is not a formal language but rather is an informal way of speaking. Hispanic Americans who use Spanglish might say things like "Vamos al movies" ("Let's go to the movies"). Or they may combine English words and phrases with Spanish words and phrases to form completely new words, such as *lonche* for "lunch" or *el mouse* for "computer mouse." Using Spanglish allows Hispanic Americans to incorporate and hold on to both sides of their identity in their daily lives. It also lets those who are not bilingual interact more easily with Spanish-speaking family members, thereby strengthening the ties between them.

ers report that they are ridiculed or treated as inferior by other Hispanics, including family members, because they are not bilingual. This can affect their self-esteem and make them question their identity. Still, although knowing Spanish helps connect Hispanics with their roots, lots of Hispanic Americans view language as just one element of their bicultural identity. In fact, the Pew Research Center reports that a majority of Hispanics say that individuals do not have to speak Spanish to be considered Latino or identify as bicultural. Writer Lola Méndez shares this point of view. She explains, "Culture goes far beyond language. My last name is Méndez and my dad was born in Uruguay. No matter which way you look at it, I am Latina, regardless of my linguistics."[26]

Family Ties

In addition to language, family ties are another important influence on how Hispanic Americans see themselves and the world around them. Hispanics hold family connections and family values in high regard. Most Hispanic families are large and tight-knit. Socializing with and being supportive of nuclear and extended family members is an integral part of Hispanic life and culture. What is more, spending time with family is a way that individuals draw closer to their cultural origins.

Many Hispanics—about 26 percent, according to a 2022 report by the Pew Research Center—live in multigenerational households. Grandparents often care for their grandchildren while the children's parents are at work. It is common for grandparents to share stories and memories of life in the family's country of origin with the children. Through this everyday interaction, older family members transmit cultural values and information about the family's heritage and history to the young.

Moreover, many Hispanic families make a point of visiting extended family in their native country, which gives young family members a chance to learn more about their roots. As Yaneth Medina, a California banker, says:

> "Family. It is one of the most important things for our Hispanic culture. It influences people and behaviors, plus it reinforces the importance of traditions and unity."[27]
>
> —Yaneth Medina, a banker

Family. It is one of the most important things for our Hispanic culture. It influences people and behaviors, plus it reinforces the importance of traditions and unity. My parents always made it a point to take me back to Mexico as a kid. We drove 40-plus hours each way to visit my family in Mexico. . . . Our trip was all about spending time with immediate family members, specifically my only living grandmother. She was a wise woman who talked about all of our traditions and made sure that we learned about our past. She was our leader and influenced and impacted all of us.[27]

Food, Holidays, and Celebrations

Memories and stories are often shared around the dinner table. Hispanic families get together every chance they get. Family get-togethers, holidays, and important events are usually celebrated with beloved American and Hispanic foods and traditions. Cus-

About a quarter of Hispanic American families live in multigenerational households. In these families, it is easy for grandparents to share family history and cultural values with the next generation.

toms and recipes are passed down from one generation to the next. Indeed, preparing and eating traditional foods and celebrating holidays and special occasions in a time-honored manner invoke memories and link people with their cultural roots. It is another way individuals hold on to and express their identity. As California culinary anthropologist Claudia Serrato explains, "Food has that power to bring you home. . . . It has the capacity to remind us and to revitalize our ancestry—our genetic memory."[28]

For Hispanic Americans most meals and celebrations combine both sides of their identity, reflecting their bicultural lives. At family barbeques, for instance, hamburgers and hot dogs are often topped with sliced green chili peppers or salsa, and depending on the family's nation of origin, side dishes are likely to include guacamole, beans, and rice. Music and intermittent dancing are not unusual. So are games like softball, potato-sack races, and *loteria*, the Hispanic version of bingo. The tradition of breaking a piñata is a standard part of Mexican American birthday parties.

American holidays, too, are celebrated in ways that honor both cultures. As LeJuan James explains:

> Although we stick to traditions, we also Hispanify each event to give it our own special twist. Take Thanksgiving, for example. At home Mami always makes the classic turkey but roasting right next to it in the oven is our beloved pernil (pork) because no holiday is right without a pernil asado [roast pork]. We usually do away with the yams, mashed potatoes, and cranberry sauce, and replace them with rice and ham, arroz con gandules [rice with peas], sliced avocado, empanadas [stuffed pastries]. . . . And instead of pies, we have flan [baked custard] and an assortment of other Puerto Rican and Dominican desserts.[29]

Bicultural Weddings

Weddings are celebrated by almost all cultures. However, there are often cultural differences in the way they are observed. For example, although modern Hispanic American weddings are like traditional American weddings in almost every way, they often feature Hispanic traditions, too. One tradition common among people of Mexican, Central American, and Puerto Rican descent is the lasso or unity ceremony. It is performed during the marriage ceremony. As the bride and groom stand at the altar, a member of the wedding party wraps a rosary in a figure eight around the couple's shoulders. The ritual symbolizes the couple being permanently joined together.

Another custom is the money dance. In this fun ritual, guests pin money on the bride or groom in order to dance with them. Since most Hispanic celebrations tend to be large and almost everyone wants to spin the newlyweds around the dance floor, the money dance can last for many songs. It is a common wedding tradition among Cubans, Mexicans, and some Central Americans.

For many couples, including these and other traditions is a way to honor their cultural heritage.

Before Christmas, many Mexican American families hold tamale-making parties, in which family members take part in the labor-intensive process of assembling the traditional holiday treats.

Similarly, Christmas dinners blend cultures and traditions. Tamales, which are little packets of cornmeal dough stuffed with savory or sweet fillings and wrapped in a corn husk or banana leaf, are frequently served along with traditional American fare. Making tamales is labor intensive. It involves a number of steps and can take a full day. Before Christmas many families hold a tamale-making party. Extended family members come from near and far to take part. Participants form an assembly line to prepare the traditional food. While they work, guests share family news and tell old and new stories. In the process, old traditions and memories are revisited, while new ones are created.

"Although we stick to traditions, we also Hispanify each event to give it our own special twist."[29]

—LeJuan James, a social media influencer

The Role of Pop Culture

Pop culture, in a variety of forms, is another way Hispanic Americans bond with each other and their bicultural heritage. Seeing

Hispanic actors, musicians, and social media influencers realistically portraying Hispanic culture helps individuals develop pride in their background and their place in American society. For example, by serving as role models, Hispanic social media influencers inspire their followers to embrace their bicultural identity. They offer advice, often in both English and Spanish, on everything from parenting and health to fashion and beauty. Some post skits and parodies about being Hispanic. Others give tutorials related to Hispanic lifestyles, including instructions on how to prepare traditional foods, salsa dance, and use Spanish slang, among other things.

Similarly, Hispanic actors and entertainers play a role in how Hispanics view themselves. Seeing celebrities who look and sound like they do and who accurately depict Hispanic culture in their work helps make Hispanics feel like they belong in and can succeed in American society. As a result, they grow more comfortable and confident about their identity. Says Ferrera, "I hear from all kinds of people that they gain confidence and self-esteem when they see themselves in the culture—a brown girl . . . an underdog, an undocumented father . . . simple portrayals that say in a resounding way, you are here, you are seen, your experience matters."[30]

Hispanic musicians, too, play an important role in helping young Hispanics see, accept, and embrace both sides of their culture. Latino hip-hop artists often rhyme in Spanglish, which is a mix of Spanish and English words and phrases. They sing and rap about things that young Hispanics can relate to. Some sing popular American hit songs that they translate into Spanish. Many collaborate with American artists, mixing Latin and American music styles to create music that reflects young Hispanic Americans' bicultural lives. The popularity of Hispanic artists such as Shakira, Pitbull, Bad Bunny, Jennifer Lopez, and J Balvin, just to name a few, gives young Hispanics a sense of pride in their culture. In this manner these artists inspire young Latinos to integrate their Hispanic heritage into their American lives. Indeed, by normalizing Hispanic culture, pop culture has helped break down barriers for young Hispanics struggling with their identity.

CHAPTER FIVE

Facing New Challenges

Hispanics have faced many challenges throughout their long history in the United States. They have made great strides in meeting these challenges. Nevertheless, new challenges continue to arise. Although Hispanic Americans can trace their roots to many nations and have had different experiences that have shaped their views on many topics, they all want the best for their children and grandchildren. Therefore, in order to ensure a better world for future generations, many individuals and groups are working hard to meet new and ongoing challenges.

Financial Empowerment

One ongoing challenge that many Hispanic Americans face is financial. Although Hispanics contribute greatly to the US economy, studies show that they lag behind White Americans financially. As a group, they earn less and have less savings but comparable debt, fewer financial assets, and inadequate credit history. All of these obstacles prevent many Hispanic Americans from building a secure financial future for themselves and their families.

There are a variety of reasons why these financial challenges exist. Not having a savings or checking account is one reason. According to the Federal Deposit Insurance Corporation, 12.2 percent of Hispanic households do not have a savings or checking account, compared to 2.5 percent of White households. Language barriers, distrust of banks among immigrants who come from countries with corrupt financial institutions, and lack of access to neighborhood banks in some communities keep many Hispanics from opening bank accounts. As a result, many turn to check-cashing businesses, which, according to financial service company Bankrate, charge fees from 1 to 12 percent of the value of a check for the service. And when Hispanic Americans need a loan, they often go to payday loan services, which have locations in many Hispanic communities. These lenders often charge as much as 400 percent interest, and many people take out one loan after another. Gary Mottola, research director of the Financial Industry Regulatory Authority, a private corporation that regulates financial markets, reports that from 2014 to 2019 Hispanics used payday loans twice as often as White people.

Even when they have savings, limited investment opportunities keep some Hispanics from growing their savings. For instance, many Hispanics do not have access to employer-sponsored retirement savings plans, which help individuals build a secure financial future. Hispanics often work in low-paying jobs or are employed by small businesses, which do not offer these plans. Or, their positions do not qualify them for their employer's retirement savings plan. In fact, the American Association of Retired Persons (AARP)

At a grand opening in Florida's Little Havana neighborhood, a bank employee assists local residents. One group has encouraged the hiring of bilingual workers to help recent immigrants from Spanish-speaking countries open accounts, get loans, and access other services.

reports that 66 percent of Hispanic workers are not covered by an employer-sponsored retirement plan. In these plans, an automatic payroll deduction is taken out of an employee's paycheck each pay period and deposited into a special retirement investment account. Since the contributions are automatically deducted from an individual's paycheck, workers are less likely to miss the money or overspend. Plus, as an employee benefit, some employers match the employee's contribution to the account with company funds. The accounts are often invested in stocks and bonds, which grow over time. Upon retirement, account holders can withdraw a lump sum or receive a monthly pension.

Many groups and individuals are taking steps to improve Latinos' financial future. Juntos Avanzamos (Together We Advance) is one. It is an organization dedicated to helping Hispanic Americans, including recent immigrants, better understand and navigate the US financial system. The organization comprises 127 credit unions, located in twenty-seven states. Bilingual bankers in these credit unions assist individuals in opening checking and savings accounts, getting loans, and accessing other financial services.

Lawmakers are helping out, too. In 2019 the state of California, as an example, established a program known as California Secure Choice. It provides workers who do not have access to a workplace retirement savings plan the opportunity to join a state-sponsored plan. Although the program serves all interested workers, Hispanic workers, who, according to the US Bureau of Labor Statistics, make up 37.7 percent of the state's labor force are a primary target of the program. Indeed, lawmakers, advocacy groups, and financial institutions are working to solve the financial challenges Hispanic Americans face, which should improve the group's current and future financial security.

Battling Climate Change

The looming threat of climate change is another new challenge Hispanic Americans are dealing with. Although climate change threatens all Americans, the majority of Hispanic Americans live in areas

American and Not American

Katie Escobar is a student at the University of Houston. She was one year old when she and her parents illegally crossed into the United States from Mexico. The United States is the only home Escobar knows. She considers herself an American. Nevertheless, as an undocumented immigrant, she has lived under the threat of deportation for almost her entire life.

In 2021, when she turned eighteen, Escobar applied for Deferred Action for Childhood Arrivals (DACA) status. DACA is a program that protects eligible undocumented immigrants—those who were brought to the United States as children—from deportation for a two-year renewable period. It also allows them to work legally and qualify for in-state college tuition. However, since its creation the legality of the program has been questioned by some lawmakers.

In July 2021 a federal judge in Texas ruled that DACA was illegal. The ruling is being appealed, but as of August 2022 DACA was not open to new applicants Escobar's application was too late. So, she and thousands of other new applicants who pinned their hopes for a stable future on DACA remain in limbo, hoping the country they call home will afford them legal status.

that are especially vulnerable to extreme weather conditions linked to climate change. Cities and towns in the Southwest, where many Hispanics make their home, experienced record-breaking heat in 2022, with temperatures reaching as high as 118°F (48°C) in Phoenix, Arizona. Adding to the problem, many Hispanic communities are located in densely populated urban neighborhoods that lack trees and green spaces that provide cooling and where roads, buildings, and air pollution trap the heat. On the hottest days, temperatures in metropolitan areas in the Southwest were higher in poor Hispanic communities than in other neighborhoods, according to a 2021 study by the University of California, Davis and the American University of Beirut. And heat is not the only climate challenge. Research conducted at the University of Arizona and the University of Kentucky shows that Hispanic coastal communities are more vulnerable to flooding caused by extreme weather than other communities. One reason is that low-income Hispanics are more likely to live in high-risk flood zones than are other Americans, mainly because housing is cheaper in flood zones. In addition, many of these communities lack proper drainage or sidewalks, which inhibit flooding. Similarly, outdated or neglected infrastructure in Hispanic communities located near rivers makes these communities vulnerable.

Considering their vulnerability, it is not surprising that a 2021 Pew Research Center poll found that 81 percent of Hispanic Americans believe that addressing climate change should be a priority, and many individuals and groups are taking steps to do so. According to Juan Roberto Madrid, an environmental science and public health specialist for the national environmental group GreenLatinos, "There has been a real national uprising in Latino activism in environmentalism in recent years. Climate change may be impacting everyone, but it is impacting Latinos more."[31]

"There has been a real national uprising in Latino activism in environmentalism in recent years. Climate change may be impacting everyone, but it is impacting Latinos more."[31]

—Juan Roberto Madrid, an environmental science and public health specialist

Creating community gardens in Hispanic neighborhoods is one way Hispanic groups and individual volunteers (pictured) are responding to rising concerns about climate change.

While groups like GreenLatinos are working with lawmakers to impact change, local groups have been planting trees, creating community gardens, and educating young people about environmental issues. Through these and other efforts, Hispanic environmental activists are hoping to make the world safer for future generations. As Tony Mada, a father who helped organized the planting of seventy-five trees at a Phoenix elementary school, confides, "I'll do anything to cool things down for my kids in this hot neighborhood."[32]

> "I'll do anything to cool things down for my kids in this hot neighborhood."[32]
>
> —Tony Mada, a Hispanic American man

Countering Extremist Groups and White Replacement Theory

Threats to safety go beyond climate change. Violence aimed at Hispanic Americans has become a topic of great concern with the rise of extremist White nationalist groups and the mainstreaming of a conspiracy theory known as the great replacement theory. The theory is based on the idea that the increasing presence of Hispanics in the United States will cause people of White European descent to become a minority in the United States while Hispanics and other people of color will gain majority status. As a result, White Americans will lose their social, cultural, economic, and political power. The theory has been spread on social media and by some right-wing news outlets and politicians. It has already led to attacks on Hispanic Americans by individuals who accept it as fact. The deadliest attack was a 2019 mass shooting that occurred at a Walmart in El Paso, Texas. The shooter killed twenty-three people and injured twenty-three others. Shortly before the shooting, he posted a manifesto online. In that posting he complained about the increase in Hispanic immigrants in Texas, calling it a Hispanic invasion; repeated divisive anti-immigration statements popular among extremist groups; and credited the great replacement theory as an inspiration for the attack. Upon his arrest, he admitted that his target was Mexican Americans.

Since the massacre, many Hispanics are plagued by persistent anxiety. As Lidia Carrillo, a Hispanic American from California, admits, "Every day when I take my daughter to school we pray. I ask God to protect her. I don't know if I'm going to see my daughter or my husband at the end of the day."[33]

To help put an end to anti-Hispanic bias and keep future generations safe, Hispanic Americans are taking a variety of steps. Many have taken a defensive stance. They have become more vigilant when they are out in public, avoiding crowded places or speaking Spanish outside their homes. Some young people have stopped wearing Mexican soccer jerseys or other apparel that might make them

> "Every day when I take my daughter to school we pray. I ask God to protect her. I don't know if I'm going to see my daughter or my husband at the end of the day."[33]
>
> —Lidia Carrillo, Hispanic American woman

Diversity in Government

Hispanics are underrepresented in local, state, and federal elected office. Despite making up more than 18 percent of the population, Hispanics make up only 1.2 percent of elected officials nationwide, reports *USA Today*. According to Inclusive America, a nonprofit organization working for diversity, equity, and inclusion in government, having more diversity in government raises the chances that all Americans will be treated equitably. An article on the organization's website explains, "No one knows the needs of a community better than the people in it. A diverse pool of leaders brings with them a set of unique experiences, opinions, and thoughts on critical issues that help enhance our government's ability to serve the needs of its entire population, especially historically disenfranchised communities."

Besides better serving diverse communities, having more diverse candidates on the ballot encourages people to participate in the political process. Research suggests that voters feel more connected to candidates like themselves. Therefore, individuals who might not otherwise vote are more apt to vote if they are offered candidates to whom they feel connected.

Inclusive America, "Why Diversity Is Important," 2022. https://inclusiveamerica.org.

a target. Others are trying to counter anti-Hispanic hate and violence by speaking out against it whenever they are confronted by it. Some are campaigning against politicians who promote the great replacement theory and organizing others to join them. And even though reforming gun laws is as controversial among Hispanics as it is among the general population, some Latino civil rights organizations such as UnidosUS are lobbying for stricter gun control laws as a way to protect Hispanic communities.

Access to Political Rights and Responsibilities

Lobbying for policies and voting for candidates who support the best interests of Hispanic communities are important ways Latinos are fighting to meet new challenges. However, having equal access to political rights and responsibilities is a growing problem for many Hispanic Americans. Hispanics are the largest minority voting bloc in the nation and are expected to be a key voting bloc in the future. But changes in the boundaries of voting districts limit their political voice. For example, redistricting in the form of gerrymandering is an illegal yet common practice that often targets minority voters. Gerrymandering involves changing an electoral district's boundaries in order to limit or favor one political party or voting bloc over another. Using tactics known as packing and cracking, Hispanic voters are packed into one congressional district in order to keep significant numbers of Hispanic voters out of other districts. Or Hispanic majority voting districts are totally eliminated, or cracked. Voters from eliminated districts are then thinly spread across dozens of districts thereby reducing the group's ability to impact the election results. As a result, gerrymandering lessens the chances of candidates being elected who understand and will fight for the best interests of Hispanic Americans. Therefore, even though Hispanic voters are becoming a larger and larger part of the population, this practice reduces their political influence.

The enactment of laws that make it more difficult to vote is another new challenge to Hispanic Americans' ability to exercise

Volunteers walk through a Hispanic neighborhood urging residents to vote. Efforts such as this, along with voter registration drives, strive to increase voter participation among Hispanic Americans.

their political rights and responsibilities. In response to unsupported claims of widespread voter fraud in the 2020 election, Republican lawmakers in many states have enacted voting restrictions. These restrictions include limiting absentee and mail-in voting and banning drive-through and twenty-four-hour voting. Many Hispanics rely on these voting methods. They often work long hours or at multiple jobs, which makes it difficult for them to get to the polls during regular voting times. Other restrictions have closed voting sites in Hispanic communities, causing long waits in the few sites that remain open or making individuals travel a long distance in order to vote. Requiring multiple forms of identification, which many Hispanics lack, is still another barrier.

As of 2022, at least nineteen states had passed voter restriction laws, and more were expected to follow. States with large Hispanic populations such as Arizona, Florida, and Texas have enacted some of the most restrictive laws. In Texas, for example, a new law makes it difficult for Spanish speakers to get help in voting, while a Florida law makes registering to vote harder. Moreover, in 2021 a Supreme Court ruling weakened the Voting Rights Act of 1965, a law that was enacted to end discrimination in voting. The ruling—which allows states to put limitations on the time, place, and manner of elections—increases the challenges Hispanic voters will face.

Gerrymandering and laws that make it more difficult to participate in elections limit the voice of Hispanic voters. Nonetheless, two proposed laws, the Freedom to Vote Act and the John Lewis Voting Rights Advancement Act, seek to curb these discriminatory practices. These acts, for example, would limit restrictions on registering to vote and would make it more difficult for states to redraw congressional voting districts in a discriminatory manner. In the meantime, Hispanic Americans continue to build their place in American society. No matter what new and future challenges lie ahead, they are ready to meet them head-on.

SOURCE NOTES

Introduction: Sixty-Two Million Strong

1. LeJuan James, *Definitely Hispanic*. New York: Atria, 2019, p. 59.
2. James, p. xii.
3. BeLatina Daily, "Latinas in the Job Market: A Force to Be Reckoned With," BeLatina, December 13, 2019. https://belatina.com.

Chapter One: Coming to America

4. Quoted in Nicole Acevedo and Isa Gutierrez, "Latinos Own and Disown 'Hispanic' in Journey to Harness Identity," NBC News, September 16, 2021. www.nbcnews.com.
5. Quoted in Made Into America, "From Poverty to Dreamland," February 15, 2022. https://madeintoamerica.org.
6. Quoted in Made Into America, "Construction Work and Guitar Player," January 21, 2022. https://madeintoamerica.org.
7. Quoted in Made into America, "'A Long Hike' for a 4 Year Old Who Becomes a Teacher," January 20, 2022. https://madeintoamerica.org.
8. Quoted in *Talk of the Nation*, "Marielitos' Stories, 30 Years After the Boatlift," NPR, July 20, 2010. www.npr.org.
9. Quoted in Virginia Sanchez Korrol, "History of Puerto Ricans in the US—Part Three," Centro, 2017. https://centropr-archive.hunter.cuny.edu.

Chapter Two: Striving for Rights

10. Quoted in America Ferrera, *American Like Me*. New York: Gallery, 2018, p. 71.
11. Quoted in Natalie Musumeci, "Border Patrol Agent Detains US Citizens for Speaking Spanish," *New York Post*, May 21, 2018. https://nypost.com.
12. Quoted in Minimalist Quotes, "Sonia Sotomayor." https://minimalistquotes.com.
13. Quoted in Immigration Legal Services of Long Island, "Latino Immigrant Wrongly Detained by ICE Will Receive $125,000," September 22, 2021. www.ilsoli.org.
14. Quoted in Immigration Legal Services of Long Island, "Latino Immigrant Wrongly Detained by ICE Will Receive $125,000."
15. Quoted in Fernanda Echavarri and Marlon Bishop, "'No Mexicans Allowed': School Segregation in the Southwest," Latino USA, March 11, 2016. www.latinousa.org.
16. Quoted in Dania Santana, "Inspirational Quotes by American Latinos," Embracing Diversity, September 23, 2019. https://embracingdiversity.us.

Chapter Three: Building Communities

17. Quoted in Edgar Cedillo, "High School Student Starts Online Newspaper for Spanish Speaking Community in Southwest Montana," KBZK, March 10, 2022. www.kbzk.com.
18. Quoted in in Paola Ramos, *Finding Latinx*. New York: Vintage, 2020, p. 226.
19. Ramos, *Finding Latinx*, p. 126.
20. Quoted in Laura Sanchez, "Baroline Is a Self-Made Woman," *Latina*. https://latina.com.
21. Ramos, *Finding Latinx*, pp. 125–26.
22. Ramos, *Finding Latinx*, p. 248.

Chapter Four: Holding On to Identity

23. Quoted in Mirtle Peña-Calderon, "Ariana DeBose on How *West Side Story* Made Her Feel Like She Was 'Enough,'" *People en Español*, March 23, 2022. https://peopleenespanol.com.
24. Quoted in Contact Music, "America Ferrera Interview," January 7, 2009. www.contactmusic.com.
25. Jatsive Hernandez, "Finding Bicultural Identity When You're Too White to Be Hispanic, Too Mexican to Be American," *Dallas (TX) Morning News*," April 15, 2018. www.dallasnews.com.
26. Lola Méndez, "What No One Tells You About Being a Latina Who Doesn't Speak Spanish," *Curiosity*, December 6, 2018. www.curiositymag.com.
27. Yaneth Medina, "Community and Family: Wintrust's Yaneth Medina Reflects on National Hispanic Heritage Month," Buffalo Grove Bank & Trust, 2022. www.buffalogrovebank.com.
28. Quoted in Anthony Rivas et al., "Through Food, Language and Dance, Latinos Preserve Their Unique Cultural Identities," ABC News, September 17, 2021. https://abcnews.go.com.
29. James, *Definitely Hispanic*, pp. 124–25.
30. Ferrera, *American Like Me*, p. xxi.

Chapter Five: Facing New Challenges

31. Quoted in Anita Snow, "Latino Activism Leads in Grassroot Efforts on Climate Change," ABC News, June 12, 2022. https://abcnews.go.com.
32. Quoted in Snow, "Latino Activism Leads in Grassroot Efforts on Climate Change."
33. Quoted in Dani Anguiano, "'It's Worse than Ever': How Latinos Are Changing Their Lives in Trump's America," *The Guardian* (Manchester, UK), October 7, 2019. www.theguardian.com.

FOR FURTHER RESEARCH

Books

Edna Acosta-Belén and Carlos E. Santiago, *Puerto Ricans in the United States: A Contemporary Portrait*. Boulder, CO: Rienner, 2018.

Jim Gallagher, *Hispanic in America*. San Diego: ReferencePoint, 2021.

Manuel G. Gonzales, *Mexicanos: A History of Mexicans in the United States*, Bloomington: Indiana University Press, 2019.

Patricia Sutton, *Asylum Seekers: Hope and Disappointment on the Border*. San Diego: ReferencePoint, 2022.

Internet Sources

Gabriela Fresquez, "Bicultural Latinos Embrace Dual Identities, Shun Pressure to Assimilate," NBC News, September 23, 2021. www.nbcnews.com.

History.com editors, "Cesar Chavez," History.com, August 25, 2022. www.history.com.

Mark D. Ramirez, "Structural Racism Against Latinos Is Part of American History," Medium, July 10, 2020. https://medium.com.

Seramount, "Latino Organizations You Need to Know," September 12, 2021. https://seramount.com.

USA Facts, "The Hispanic Population Has Quadrupled in the Past Four Decades. It Is Also Becoming More Diverse," April 18, 2022. https://usafacts.org.

Websites

Centro
https://centropr-archive.hunter.cuny.edu
Centro is the name given to the Center for Puerto Rican Studies, a research center located at Hunter College in New York City. It studies all aspects of Puerto Rican life in the United States and provides a wide range of articles about Puerto Rican history, culture, and experiences.

Daily Chela

www.dailychela.com

This digital media outlet provides articles, podcasts, and essays about Hispanic American life, culture, art, history, and politics. It also offers a digital streaming service.

National Parks Service

www.nps.gov/subjects/tellingallamericansstories/latinothemestudy.htm

The section titled "American Latino Heritage Theme Study" on the National Parks Service website provides a wide range of articles about Hispanic life in the United States.

Pew Research Center

www.pewresearch.org

The Pew Research Center is a nonpartisan think tank. It conducts research and opinion polls and provides information on social issues, demographic trends, and public opinion on all sorts of topics, including numerous issues concerning Hispanic Americans.

UnidosUS

www.unidosus.org

UnidosUS is the largest Latino civil rights organization in the United States. It offers articles and videos on its website about civil rights, health, education, immigration, and financial issues, among other subjects affecting Hispanic Americans.

INDEX

PICTURE CREDITS

Sources: Hispanic Americans by the Numbers

- Nicholas Jones, et al., "Improved Race and Ethnicity Measures Reveal U.S. Population Is Much More Multiracial," U.S. Census, August 12, 2021. www.census.gov.
- USA Facts, "The Hispanic Population Has Quadrupled in the Past Four Decades. It Has Also Become More Diverse," April 18, 2022. https://usafacts.org.
- US Census Bureau, "Census Bureau Releases New Educational Attainment Data," February 24, 2022. www.census.gov.
- Elizabeth Arias, et al., "United States Life Tables, 2020," National Vital Statistics Reports, August 8, 2022. www.cdc.gov/nchs/data/nvsr/nvsr71/nvsr71-01.pdf.
- Jens Manuel and Luis Noe-Bustamante, "Key facts about U.S. Latinos for National Hispanic Heritage Month," Pew Research Center, September 9, 2021. www.pewresearch.org.
- Statista, "Hispanic Population of the United States in 2019," Statista Research Department, January 27, 2022. www.statista.com.